Managing
GENERATION Y

*Global Citizens Born in the
Late Seventies and Early Eighties*

Bruce Tulgan
Carolyn A. Martin, Ph.D.

HRD PRESS
Amherst, Massachusetts

Copyright © 2001, RainmakerThinking, Inc.

Published by: HRD Press, Inc.
                 22 Amherst Road
                 Amherst, MA 01002
                 800-822-2801 (U.S. and Canada)
                 413-253-3488
                 413-253-3490 (fax)
                 http://www.hrdpress.com

Printed in Canada

ISBN: 0-87425-622-4

Cover design by Eileen Klockars
Editorial and production services by Mary George

Dedicated to all Gen Yers
whose voices ring out loud and true in this book
and to the managers everywhere
who will coach these global citizens

–Contents

– Acknowledgments

As always, we must thank first and foremost the many thousands of incredible people who, over the years, have shared the lessons of their experiences through Rainmaker-Thinking's ongoing workplace-interview research. At the top of our list for this project are all the Generation Yers across North America who took the time to tell us their stories. They are the heartbeat of this book and deserve our special thanks.

We are also indebted to the many others who lent their assistance to the research for *Managing Generation Y,* especially the following: Christie Duncan, Jeanne Yerko-vich, and the staff of the School-to-Work Program at David Douglas High School, in Portland, Oregon, who allowed us to interview their positive, upbeat Gen Yers; the research assistants at RainmakerThinking, notably Jeff Hockenbrock, Kelly Poggio, and Heather Neely, each of whom contributed several dozen in-depth interview transcripts and who collected most of the transcripts excerpted in this book; Cynthia Conrad at Rainmaker-Thinking, who compiled the recommended resources appendix and whose regular research and editing contributes so much to all of our publications.

To the rest of our colleagues at RainmakerThinking, especially Jeff Coombs, Mark Kurber, Peggy Urbanowicz, Colleen Keating, and Susan Ciemniewski, thank you for your hard work and the valuable contributions you make to this enterprise every day.

Many thanks as well to our friend and publisher, Bob Carkhuff, and his staff at HRD Press. Bob has continuously supported our work since the early days, when it was a gamble. The partnership we maintain with HRD Press is critical to our ability to reach inside organizations of every shape and size and make them even better than they already are. Special thanks, too, to Mary George for her editing and design work.

To all of the business leaders and managers who have expressed so much confidence in our work, thank you for giving us the opportunity to learn from the real management issues you must deal with and solve on a daily basis. Thanks especially to Dick Bristol, retail support manager at the Ace Hardware Distribution Center in Rocklin, California, for modeling what it means to be a great boss and team player; and to Sherrie Barger, principal of Gilbert Heights Elementary School, Portland, Oregon, who inspired our "Declaration of Respect."

Finally, as co-authors, we also have our respective debts of gratitude to express. From Carolyn: Thank you to Kathy Richard, who thoughtfully read and re-read this manuscript and provided much encouragement, love, and support. From Bruce: Thank you to my family and friends, for being you and for allowing me to be who I am; and as always, I reserve my deepest thanks for my wife, Debby Applegate, who is my best friend, my partner in all things, and owner of my heart.

–Introduction

HERE THEY COME: the members of the fourteenth American generation. They're self-confident and optimistic. Independent and goal-oriented. Masters of the Internet and PC. Young adults who believe education is cool, integrity is admirable, and parents are role models.

They're blunt. They're savvy. They're contradictory. They defy easy labeling and exact parameters. They're the children of the baby boomers, the upbeat younger siblings of Generation X, and the 29 million young adults who have been streaming into the workplace over the last five years and whose presence will continue to grow every single year for the next decade.

Demographers, unable to agree on a defining label for this generation, have called them the Millenniums, Generation www, the Digital Generation, Generation E, Echo Boomers, N-Gens, and, most often, Generation Y. Ask these young people to define themselves, though, and you will hear something far more creative: the Non-Nuclear Family Generation, the Nothing-Is-Sacred Generation, the Wannabes, the Feel Good Generation, CyberKids, the Do-or-Die Generation, the Searching-for-an-Identity Generation.

This "labeling challenge" was aptly described by one 22-year-old in following way:

> *You can't name a generation like ours as easily as others, because we aren't as easy to typecast as the boomers or Gen X. Maybe we should be called 'X-Squared,' since our lives seem to be so much more diverse than that of our predecessors.*

But perhaps the challenge was best summarized by a 20-year-old who bluntly said, "I think my generation has jumped through hoops and broken backs to ensure that no names 'fit' it."

As authors who respect our subjects, we found ourselves in somewhat of a quandary when it came to identifying, with an appropriate moniker, this generation for our book. We were well aware that Generation X had been named by advertising executives bent on using one catch-all term to capture 52 million young people, and we did not want to encourage a replay of history. Thus we began calling the new generation "North Americans born in the late seventies and early eighties," and later amended that to "Global citizens born in the late seventies and early eighties" ("GCBLSEEs")—a more fitting title, as this is the first generation to come of age in a truly global society.

However, it soon became clear that the media had settled on the much catchier "Generation Y," and so, as uncomfortable as we are with that, we have used "Generation Y" as a convenient shorthand, with utmost apologies to all the CyberKids, Wannabes, and N-Gens subsumed in this category.

Demographers have also been unable to agree on the new generation's exact parameters. Those who refer to Gen Yers as "Echo Boomers," children of the baby boomers, identify this generation as a huge one, spanning 20 years from 1978 to 1998. Others cut the gap to 10 years, defining Gen Yers as those born between 1978 and 1988. Both views are problematic.

Since a generation is an identifiable age group with a shared historical experience, the time span of each new generation shortens as the pace of change accelerates. The baby boom spans 17 to 19 years, beginning in 1946 and ending anywhere from 1962 to 1964, depending on the source. Generation X, by the broadest definition, spans only 15 years (1963 to 1977), and only 13 years for those who put the first birth year of Xers at 1965. If we are to define the next generational group, or cohort, in any meaningful way, the time span must be shorter still, no more than seven years. That is why we have focused this study on those born between 1978 and 1984.

The young adults who were born in this time span—call them GCBLSEEs or Gen Yers—make up the next cohort in RainmakerThinking's ongoing study of the working

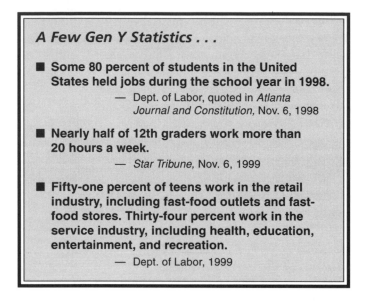

A Few Gen Y Statistics . . .

■ **Some 80 percent of students in the United States held jobs during the school year in 1998.**
— Dept. of Labor, quoted in *Atlanta Journal and Constitution,* Nov. 6, 1998

■ **Nearly half of 12th graders work more than 20 hours a week.**
— *Star Tribune,* Nov. 6, 1999

■ **Fifty-one percent of teens work in the retail industry, including fast-food outlets and fast-food stores. Thirty-four percent work in the service industry, including health, education, entertainment, and recreation.**
— Dept. of Labor, 1999

lives of people born after 1963. So far, our interview research on this particular cohort has focused primarily on North Americans. That research, as well as our work with hundreds of companies in just about every industry, forms the basis of this pocket guide, the latest in our series published by HRD Press.

The Gen Yers we interview every day range from 16- to 22-year-olds. They are high school juniors and seniors and college-aged young adults, virtually all of whom are busy compiling impressive resumes before hitting the full-time workplace. Many have three or four part-time job experiences or internships under their belts, and most are already sure they know what they want out of their careers and how they want to be managed.

Over and over again, in their unique voices, different Gen Yers say the same things about workplace issues—as if someone had given hundreds of young adults from all over the country, from different ethnic and socioeconomic backgrounds, "the answers to the test." As you will see demonstrated in this book, they are bluntly articulate about the worst bosses they've ever had and highly respectful of the best. They revel in an independent "get off my back" attitude, and are perfectly poised to extend—and accelerate—into the twenty-first century the workplace trends started in the 1990s by their Gen-X siblings.

While it's risky to draw too many conclusions about the working lives of young people, many of whom are still teenagers, one thing is certain: These 29 million young people will make the next major impact on the workplace. Already they're posing new challenges to business leaders and managers, who are spending more time, more energy, and more money than ever before recruiting and training the young talent they need to compete in today's high-speed, high-tech world.

The purpose of this book is to help you understand who Generation Yers really are, so you can bring out the best in the new vanguard from their very first days in the workforce and throughout their young adulthood. If you are positioned to meet the challenges they bring to the workplace—if you are willing to implement some of the best practices we've identified to keep Gen Yers engaged and motivated—you will take a quantum leap ahead of your competition.

1.

Who Is Generation Y?

YOU WOULD THINK the mainstream media had learned a lesson from its early stereotype of Gen Xers as slackers and cynical mopes; but judging from most of its coverage of Generation Y, it did not. Gen Yers are typically portrayed as lazy, self-interested kids constantly at risk for drugs, sex, and violence. At best, they are pampered and ill-mannered; at worst, they are hopelessly derelict.

Why is the media so worried about Generation Y?

Gen Yers grew up amid the specters of crack cocaine, designer drugs, and the AIDS epidemic. As 8- to 14-year-olds, they saw the graphic horrors of the L.A. riots following the Rodney King verdict and the fiery end of the Branch Davidian standoff. They watched terrorism become a U.S. phenomenon with the World Trade Center, Oklahoma City, and Atlanta Summer Olympics bombings. They were bombarded with violence-packed video games and sexually charged advertising, TV, and movies. Then, in the late '90s, they were implicated as a disturbed and violent generation when the school shootings at Paducah, Littleton, Springfield, and Conyers grabbed the headlines.

Gen Yers didn't need the atom bomb or nuclear proliferation to feel that the world was an uncertain, scary place. They didn't need a Second World War or a Korea or a Vietnam to feel terrified. Their "war" was fought on native soil. Their "enemy" appeared in their homes, in their neighborhoods, on their playgrounds: in adults who sought to abuse them; in schoolmates who might suddenly shoot them.

Graphic news stories present Gen Yers as a scary group of teens driven by adult desires, problems, and weapons, but without the faculties to cope. Is this the reality, though? Robert Blum, head of the adolescent health program at the University of Minnesota, assures us that it is not: We might expect Gen Y to be "a profoundly violent generation. But it's not there."

It's not there. The fact is, the majority of Gen Yers are coping quite well, thank you. Moreover, they've made great strides since their elder siblings made it through the teen years. Look at the evidence:

- Teen arrests are down.
- Teen drug use is down.
- Teen drunk-driving accidents are down.

- Teen pregnancy is down.
- Teen abortions are down.
- High school dropout rates are down.

Indeed, Gen Y may very well prove to be the "best generation" yet in the United States (see below).

Maybe the Best Generation . . .

It's time to see our kids for who they truly are. Most of them are not rude, wild, and irresponsible; in fact, most of them could one day make this country an immensely better place.
— David Gergen, Editor at Large, *U.S. News*

The future will be grand because our kids will be its keepers. . . . [This generation] is more interesting, more confident, less hidebound and uptight, better educated, more creative, and, in some essential fashion, unafraid. . . . [My own children are] simply better than I was at their age, [and their peers are] generous in ways unknown to me when I was young.
— Anna Quindlen, in *Newsweek* (Jan. 2000)

These are goodhearted kids, and when you give them the opportunity to have responsibility, they run with it.
— Adraine LaRoza, Executive Director, Volunteer Services of Manatee County, Florida, and overseer, ManaTEENClub

[They have] not just better attitudes and behaviors than we have a right to expect, but an optimism and responsibility that leave elders' empty moralisms in the dust.
— Mike A. Males, *Framing Youth* (1999)

I think you could argue that they are the best we've had.
— Samuel Halperin, Senior Fellow, American Youth Policy Forum

THE TRUTH ABOUT GENERATION Y

We can describe Gen Yers in four positive ways as:

1. *A generation of new confidence, upbeat and full of self-esteem*

2. *The most education-minded generation in history*

3. *A generation paving the way to a more open, tolerant society*

4. *A generation leading a new wave of volunteerism*

These are truths that cut through the fictions and give us the real Gen Y.

GEN Y TRUTH 1. A Generation of New Confidence, Upbeat and Full of Self-Esteem

Because Gen Yers are coming of age during the most consistently expansive economy in the last 30 years, they have a more optimistic outlook on life, work, and the future than Xers did at their age. Most studies show that up to 80 percent of Gen Yers believe they will be financially better off than their parents. Contrast that with their older siblings, who were told they would be the first generation in U.S. history to be financially worse off than their parents.

Gen Yers have emerged from the shadow of the fiercely independent Gen Xers to take their place as the "self-esteem generation." That self-esteem is not too surprising, for Yers grew up basking in "The Decade of the Child," a time when humanistic theories of childhood psychology permeated counseling, education, and parenting. And don't forget, in the '90s, parents worked double-time to get the balancing act right, after the workaholic '80s. Also, a growing number of businesses extended parental leave to men as well as women, and fathers became more involved in parenting than ever before.

Sure, there are plenty of Gen Yers who are angry about parental "absenteeism" caused by divorce or the demands of a dual-income household. Yet, according to a *Newsweek* poll (May 2000), 61 percent of teenagers say their parents spend enough time with them (15 percent say they spend too much time). And an extensive study of the Class of 2000 found that 46 percent of high school seniors feel they have an "excellent" relationship with their parents, up from 34 percent who felt that way as freshmen (study reported by the CBS news show, *48 Hours*).

Although we may attribute Gen Y's confidence to self-esteem-building parenting, education, and counseling, we must also acknowledge the unique role technology has played in strengthening that confidence. Gen Yers' facility with technology has empowered them in ways older cohorts can only imagine. This digital generation has never experienced life without computers. In fact, many of them were booting up computers long before they were hopping on bikes.

Techno-savvy Yers are now usurping "intellectual authority" in their homes and classrooms, leaving parents and teachers both confused and awed. They can access worlds of information and master increasingly complex systems much faster than their elders. They're consultants to parents who don't know how to use technology, and collaborators with teachers, infusing technology into the curriculum. They're proud owners of impressive electronic portfolios filled with website designs, home pages, and Internet resource guides. They know how to use the Internet as efficiently as older generations used the library, but in this case, gaining *instant* access to people, events, and ideas.

This technology-bolstered confidence was well expressed by a 21-year-old intern at a nonprofit organization:

> *My current boss usually manages my work in whatever way I suggest, because she recognizes that she does not have the expertise to contradict me. Her expertise is in public policy, not IT. She describes the ends that she wants the technology in the office to create; then she leaves me relatively free to implement her vision.*

Imagine having a young intern in your company tell you that!

Gen Yers are wired for the future. Slow, unwieldy processes are out; streamlining is in. "One size fits all" is out; customization of anything is in. Passive learning is out; interactivity is in.

The Most Education-Minded Generation in History

Influenced by parents who value education and a workplace that demands it, most Gen Yers recognize that the key to their success lies in advanced learning:

- Ninety percent of high school seniors expect to attend college.

- Seventy percent of them expect to work in professional jobs.

- Seventy percent of teens believe college is necessary to meet their career goals.

- Forty percent of college freshmen expect to get their master's degrees.

As a result, more high school students than ever before are taking harder college-prep courses. This "education is cool" generation views lifelong education as a fact of life.

The good news for recent college grads is that their talents are in great demand and starting salaries continue to rise. JobTrak.com reports that for the Class of 2000 salaries rose anywhere from $600 per year at the low end (in the communications and media fields) to $3400 per year at the high end (in computer technology and information sciences fields).

Although 1.2 million of the 3.3 million Gen Yers born in 1978 received college degrees in 2000, part-time college and university students are the new majority on many campuses. The line between school and work has become blurred. Colleges offer students credit for work experience, more and more college and university courses are being offered online, and distance learning has lost its stigma and is now regarded as cutting edge. Meanwhile, more and more organizations are developing their own in-house "universities," while others partner with traditional universities in education programs, sometimes paying for their employees' college credits. Some employers even negotiate college credits for their own training courses.

These changes in education have even made inroads into the U.S. Army, which traditionally has only offered education "hiring bonuses" to be used *after* years of service. In an attempt to halt the exodus of its best talent, the Army recently instituted a program that will soon allow soldiers to earn college degrees or technical certifications *during* their four-year active enlistment, through a system based on distance learning. No matter where soldiers are stationed, they'll be able to access classes online, at any time. As Secretary of the Army Louis Caldera explained, "What we want to do is [offer more than] an either-or choice. You can learn while you serve."

Organizations of all kinds are increasingly willing to accommodate education-minded Gen Yers. For example, take Enterprise Rent-A-Car. This company "saved" a rising star from defecting to academia when they learned he wanted to study for an MBA. How? They offered to pay for his program and assured him that he would have the flexible schedule needed to complete his course work. The young man didn't have to make an either-or choice. He could earn and learn. And the organization retained a good employee.

Whether you offer Gen Yers the opportunity to get their GEDs or Ph.D.s, they're turned on by organizations committed to their lifelong learning. For these young people, education is something that spans boundaries of place and time, and they will do most of their learning in a self-paced way, "just in time" to meet the knowledge gaps in their real lives and work.

GEN Y TRUTH 3. A Generation Paving the Way to a More Open, Tolerant Society

As the children of biracial and multicultural marriages, creators of customized spiritual paths, and railers against racism, sexism, and homophobia, Gen Yers are the most pluralistic, integrated generation in U.S. history—and the best hope we've had so far for a more open, tolerant society. Led by icons like Tiger Woods and Mariah Carey, young adults are struggling to define themselves beyond the traditional confines of race, religion, and ethnicity; the more self-confident among them are not only growing in self-acceptance but also opening the way to "other-acceptance."

Of course, the slurs, the insults, the ostracism still exist. Gen Yers are, after all, heirs to a deeply divided society. But, as one 17-year-old student, quoted in *Newsweek* (May 8, 2000), says of racial divisions, "people don't trip on it so much now." Why are these young adults not "tripping" so much on the differences that divided their parents' and grandparents' generations? Perhaps in part because one in three of them is a non-white minority. In fact, Gen Y will be the first generation to grow old as the white population of the United States becomes a minority.

Most Gen Yers think it's downright stupid to judge people based solely on their gender, heritage, or sexual orientation. They say, resoundingly, that talent, and no other factor, should be the key to success. Consequently, they often form close bonds of loyalty with those who share their differences as well as honor their uniqueness. Technology has made it possible for them to establish and maintain closer relationships with people who share similar interests than with those who merely share the same neighborhood. And in cyberspace, the differences that once divided people are simply not defining issues.

A Generation Leading a New Wave of Volunteerism

Right now, we are witnessing the coming of age of the most socially conscious generation since the '60s. In response to messages from schools, homes, and churches that they can make a difference, Gen Yers are exhibiting a refreshing altruism that embraces environmental, socioeconomic, and community problems.

From toy drives to working for better child labor laws; from supporting local recycling programs to calling for corporate ecological standards; from traveling to India to work with Mother Teresa's community to volunteering at local food banks to distribute groceries; from raising money for breast cancer research to saving music and arts programs in local high schools, Gen Yers are contributing in record numbers.

For example, look at the ManaTEENClub in Manatee County, Florida, one of the nation's largest youth volunteer organizations. Ten thousand teens donate more than a million hours of service a year, helping out in soup kitchens, working as tutors, repairing mobile homes for the elderly, and otherwise making a difference in their communities. That's an average of 100 hours of service per teen per year.

Colleges and universities are supporting and further encouraging this altruistic spirit. For instance, George Fox University in Newberg, Oregon, shuts down completely for one day each year so students, faculty, and staffers can contribute to service projects throughout the city. Indeed, colleges all across the country are bridging the chasm between "town and gown" by engaging students in "service learning." The trend is to go beyond academics to mold young adults into socially conscious, aware citizens. And it's working. UCLA's annual national survey reports that a record-high 75 percent of college freshman performed volunteer work in 1999.

This same volunteer impulse beats strongly through Gen Y high schoolers. Rebecca George, Associate Dean of Admissions at Albertus Magnus College in New Haven, Connecticut, interviews thousands of high school students every year. She reports that volunteerism and community service are "huge" among students, who "indicate their involvement with their neighborhoods, local service groups, church activities, Boy Scout–style clubs in numbers that their siblings could never compete with."

Clearly, Gen Yers are far more than what so many in the media would like to make of them.

GEN Y AND THE CHALLENGE FOR ORGANIZATIONS

We are about to see what happens when the workforce is inundated by talented, educated, techno-savvy, open-minded, service-oriented young people with every intention of making lots of money while building their ideal careers and personal lives. Will your organization be able to deliver the dream job Gen Yers are looking for?

Keep in mind that, *first,* Gen Yers' career choices and behavior are driven primarily by their quest for a chance to play meaningful roles in meaningful work that helps others. In essence, they want to be "paid volunteers"—to join an organization not because they have to, but because they really want to, because there's something significant happening there.

For example, a 21-year-old machinist is excited about working in an electrical shop precisely because "it's an environment where you can produce something useful, and you can see people glad that they've got this piece of equipment that never existed before. It's magic to them."

The "magic" for Gen Yers comes in making a difference—in producing something worthwhile—while working with a great team and getting the rewards they feel they have earned.

Second, Gen Yers want to be part of a highly motivated team of committed people. They like working closely with and learning from colleagues they respect, and they hope to socialize and even form friendships with their co-workers. Those human connections are what makes work fun for Generation Y.

Why is collaborating with a dedicated community of people so important to Gen Yers? Perhaps in part because they spend a lot of time alone. Despite hours on the Internet, extracurricular activities, and mall hopping with their friends, Gen Yers still spend up to 20 percent of their time by themselves. Spending a lot of time alone helps a person develop a tremendous level of independence, but it also stimulates a craving for connections.

Also, with experience in team-focused classrooms, sports arenas, church groups, and volunteer organizations, Yers are poised to be great team players, with a very different style of teamwork than Gen Xers. Whereas Gen Xers want to be part of a team of sole proprietors who meet to put their individual contributions together in a sum that is greater than its parts, Gen Yers prefer working side by side with energized and energizing co-workers.

Thus, making people of all backgrounds feel welcomed, mobilizing their unique talents to get important work done, and aggressively creating an open and open-minded workplace are major challenges for every organization.

Third, Gen Yers have lofty financial and personal goals, and fully expect to meet them. Most surveys of Gen Yers report that they expect to earn very high salaries by the time they are 30. Considering that the average starting salary of a college graduate in 2000 hovered around $38,000, and that more and more organizations are figuring out ways to "flex" schedules, work locations, and job descriptions, Gen Yers may be more realistic in their expectations than those who scoff at their ambition.

And therein lies a dilemma. Until 2005, most jobs available to Gen Yers will be minimum-wage positions that meet none of their expectations. Currently, they hold jobs that few others want, working in the fast-food industry or as store clerks, baby sitters, yard workers, and so on. It should come as no surprise, then, that so many of the most promising teenagers in the workforce often become bored and isolated and feel little incentive to excel. It's no wonder that offers of slight increases in hourly wages will lure them out your door and across the street to work for your competitors.

That's why you must figure out a way to offer Gen Yers incentives at work that few competitors are willing or able to offer. Money matters a lot, but Yers are willing to meet specific work standards—goals, deadlines, and parameters—in exchange for the financial and nonfinancial rewards they seek.

2.

What Can Managers Expect from Generation Y?

WHEN YOU MEET GEN YERS, in interviews or team meetings, behind the store counter or in the cubicle next to yours, what should you expect? Granted that on an individual level Gen Yers can be quite different from one another, in general there are several characteristics that distinguish their cohort from others. And not too surprisingly, they share some similarities with their Gen X siblings while clearly exhibiting their own distinctive generational mark.

WHAT TO EXPECT . . .

Like their Gen X siblings, Gen Yers are independent, techno-savvy, entrepreneurial hard workers who thrive on flexibility. But in every way, they take these qualities to new heights or transform them:

> ➡ *Gen Yers are comfortably self-reliant.* You will find, in place of Gen Xers' fierce independence, a self-reliance that is less reactionary than

"matter of fact." As we will see later, this links up well with the Gen Y attraction to teamwork.

➤ *Gen Yers want technology—and everything else—right now.* Gen Xers are in a hurry, no doubt; they want to know what you have to offer them next week. But Gen Yers want to know what you have to offer them *right now.*

Remember, whereas Gen X grew up witnessing Moore's Law—"Technology doubles every two years"—in action, by the time Gen Y was entering its teenage years, technology was beginning to outpace that law. Most Gen Yers have been using computers since preschool and can dazzle the greatest techies of Gen X; with that skill comes an expectation of immediacy.

➤ *Gen Yers want infinitely thrilling opportunities.* While Gen X thrives on new experience, Gen Y demands thrill—and, as we will see, not just the "extreme sports" brand of thrill. Because of many factors in their upbringing, Gen Yers are natural entrepreneurs, eager for responsibility and attuned to innovation.

In many ways, Gen Y is like Gen X on fast forward with self-esteem. Understanding these characteristics, and the challenges they pose, will you give the edge in learning how to manage Gen Y.

➡ Gen Yers Are Comfortably Self-Reliant

Like Xers, Yers are a "latchkey" generation. With our country's high divorce rate and dual-income families, many have been left to their own devices and taught to take care of themselves. Yet because they have also been reared on the discourse of self-esteem, Gen Yers are far less fierce than Xers in their independence and more comfortable and self-assured. Their matter-of-fact, "of course I can fend for myself" style is thus quite different from the intense Gen X, "I'd better be able to fend for myself; now get out of my way." Gen Yers' strong desire for collaboration adds another dimension: They want to do things their own way, but they work most enthusiastically in teams.

Unlike their under-supervised Gen X siblings, many Yers have grown up over-supervised. Their parents enrolled them in time-intensive before- and after-school activities, and bound them to the technological tethers of pagers and cell phones. Gen Yers have been so micromanaged by their parents, teachers, and counselors that now they're eager to manage their own time. That means managers should be prepared to coach Gen Yers in time management skills—how to break up large projects into more manageable pieces, plan their time, handle day-to-day tasks and responsibilities in the midst of interruptions, and meet deadlines—so they won't have to put up with managers breathing down their necks.

A 21-year-old office assistant in a real estate firm speaks for her generation when she says:

> *I definitely don't want someone breathing down my neck. . . . I like to be given [a task and allowed] to do it at my own pace, and I will get it done.*

You will find Yers asking, almost in the same breath, for help, for advice, and for partners in everything from brainstorming to execution. A 17-year-old self-described "go-fer" for a recording studio praised his manager

> *because she would tell me what job needed to be done and then let me do it. She wouldn't explain for hours how to do it, and she let me get right to it. I had to figure out the best way to do the job.*

You will also find that Gen Yers love to be assigned a challenge (the results you need), given some freedom to explore the challenge, and then matched to the best team to tackle the challenge.

A multinational pharmaceutical company recently told us they had just hired 20 graduates from the same university. Their strategy was to provide new hires with ready-made friendship groups and support systems to ease their transition into the workplace.

What's *your* strategy?

➡ Gen Yers Want Technology—and Everything Else—*Right Now*

An ad for a high-tech company shows a youngster sitting at a computer, head in hands, completely exasperated. The caption reads: "The average Internet download takes 22 seconds. That's 22 seconds longer than a 10-year-old wants to wait." The pace of everything continues to accelerate. To a Gen Yer, every second is a stretch, a year is long term, and three years is just a mirage.

This generation won't be lured by promises of climbing ladders, paying dues, and cashing out at retirement. They want to know:

- What value can I add today?
- What can I learn today?
- What will you offer me today?
- How will I be rewarded today?

Organizations that can't—or won't—customize training, career paths, incentives, and work responsibilities need a wake-up call.

Of course, youthful impatience is something common to every generation as it comes of age. But Yers often exhibit a distinctive, healthy impatience when their tasks and responsibilities are at stake. They're asking, "How can I do my job when I don't have the training, resources, and information I need to pull it off?"

You can count on this: Gen Yers will be curious not only about your culture, mission, and goals, your products, services, and customers, your compensation and benefits, but also about the technology you use to support them. Yers have high expectations of technology, and when it doesn't measure up, they get impatient. They want to know:

- Does your organization have the systems in place to get vital information to people just in time, any time, every time people need it?

- Do you have the cutting-edge equipment required to compete in the global economy?

- Do you have a variety of training resources to match their multimedia learning style?

- Do you encourage techno-savvy people to use their skills to assist less technologically adept colleagues?

➡ Gen Yers Want Infinitely Thrilling Opportunities

Gen X was touted as the most entrepreneurial generation in American history—that is, until Gen Y came along. Today it's not twenty-something business leaders capturing headlines, but teenagers. Encouraged by their Gen X predecessors and often financed by their baby-boomer parents, Gen Yers are starting their own businesses in record numbers—from employment services to teen Web shows to incredibly successful dotcoms—and often doing it while they're still in high school.

The high schools themselves are encouraging such moves. Many are expanding onsite opportunities for budding entrepreneurs, including businesses in computers, construction, catering, design and manufacturing, day care, and art sales. For example, take St. Helens High School in St. Helens, Oregon. Housing nine different businesses, this school boasts of running the only JC Penney catalog store in the country managed by high school students.

On the other hand, there are Gen Yers like the 21-year-old owner of a janitorial service whom we met in California. Married at 14, divorced at 20, she had already created one successful company in Idaho and was moving in with her sister so she could replicate her enterprise in Northern California. We were intrigued by her business method: She does none of the janitorial work herself, but, instead, outsources day-to-day projects to local people as well as the just-in-time delivery of cleaning supplies to her client sites. Her responsibilities are marketing, paying bills, and issuing paychecks. When we asked her how she learned to do that, she explained:

My parents were restaurateurs, very entrepreneurial people. So I decided not to go to college and sit in business classes and just learn theory. I tapped my

> *parents' expertise and talked to every successful*
> *business owner I could find in my town. Then I*
> *just did what they did.*

This leads us to another vital point about Yers: They will always need the wisdom of older, seasoned mentors. And they crave the guidance of knowledgeable, confident managers and co-workers. But they also want their valuable contributions appreciated—they want their ideas to be heard by expert listeners who don't outright discount Yers simply because they're young. Gen Yers are not only outside-the-box thinkers; they are innovative over-the-wall doers who won't settle for one-size-fits-all solutions.

Don't be surprised when Yers unrelentingly ask you *"Why?"* Gen Yers challenge everything. Don't get miffed when they throw an "of course, there are other ways to do this" attitude at you. This constant questioning is the product of lifelong exposure to the diverse viewpoints and infinite possibilities presented by technology and the information tidal wave. Gen Yers have been bombarded by endless choices and options. They've been challenged by diverse core beliefs, opinions, and points of view. They're often unwilling to settle for one solution until others have been explored. And that is, of course, the prerequisite for innovation.

If you've been complaining that none of your staffers seem willing to accept more responsibility, then listen to the complaint of this 18-year-old salesclerk:

> [Employers] never give you the chance to prove
> yourself as a valuable employee. It was apparent to
> me that no one cared enough to say, "Okay, you've
> proven that you can do this really well. Now let's see
> if you can do this." I felt the need to grow and to
> be trusted with more responsibility [because I knew
> I could do it], but some never gave me the chance. I
> always hated that.

A 21-year-old language teacher told us about a manager
who tapped that Gen Y desire for more responsibility:

> I was the only person helping the boss—he didn't
> have any other employees. He left on vacation two
> weeks into my internship, and I became him. And
> it was infinitely thrilling because I had never really
> held a job with any kind of responsibility before. I
> got to interact with all his friends and associates.
> They didn't know how young I was.

You don't have to send Gen Yers skateboarding acrobat-
ically around town, kayaking out of a "hole," or surfing
slopes or waves to supply them with thrills. Unless you're
in the extreme-sports business, stick to the work at hand.
Yers may be addicted to the feeling of rushing adrenaline,
but the work itself can be infinitely thrilling when they
know they can say, "I did this myself" and "I am pushing
the envelope." Your goal is to grab hold of the context

of those sentiments: "I did this myself *at work*" and "I am pushing the envelope *at work*."

EXPECT THE BEST FROM GEN Y, AND THAT'S WHAT YOU'LL GET

Are we looking at Gen Y through rose-colored glasses? We don't think so.

Of course, some Gen Yers are violent, bigoted, and disrespectful. Of course, some are irresponsible and will never contribute anything meaningful to life. But those youngsters are far and few between and hardly the most noteworthy segment of Generation Y.

Our research has focused on the broad trends and vast majority of this emerging generation, and it has found talented young adults eager to make a difference and seeking adult role models to help them on their way. An old saw claims, "You get what you expect." The best parents, the best educators, and the best leaders have always known that.

Leaders like D. Michael Abrashoff, naval commander of the U.S.S. Benfold, know it. Abrashoff has transformed hundreds of Gen Y recruits—most from economically deprived homes, some already involved in drugs and gangs—into the most highly trained, efficient combat crew in the fleet. How does he do that? He expects them to be grassroots leaders—and they rise to his expectation. He expects them to be smart, talented, and dedicated—and they deliver. He expects them to contribute astonishing ideas to raise morale—and they do.

Educators like Lorraine Monroe know it too. Principal Monroe transformed Harlem's Intermediate School 10 (known for violence, high absenteeism, and low achievement) into the Frederick Douglass Academy, one of the top schools in New York City. How did she do that? She formulated "Twelve Non-Negotiable Rules and Regulations"—each one based on respect—and expected every teacher and student to follow them. And they did. The result? In 1996, 96 percent of Frederick Douglass students went on to college.

As Yers continue to make inroads into the workplace, the balance will gradually shift from boomer-dominated values and structures to those defined by Gen X and Gen Y—and, synchronistically, those demanded by the new economy. Together, these two generations are now redefining how organizations can get the best work done by the best talent. Gen X and Gen Y already make up nearly half of the American workforce, 55 million strong. More than 14 million Gen Yers are already active in the U.S. workforce today. In fact, the rate of teens working in the United States is the highest in the industrialized world, and the highest in recorded U.S. history.

Both Gen X and Gen Y witnessed the demise of the lifetime employment paradigm their grandparents retired from and their parents were disillusioned by. After the tumultuous '80s and early '90s, when businesses told the workforce, "You're no longer our business. You're on your own," free agency became the wave of the future. And people of all ages are riding it today.

This trend will hold true for Generation Y. Whether working for themselves or others, Gen Yers have become the owners of what Tom Peters calls "Me, Inc." The best young talent is learning to negotiate the best deals in ways older generations would never have conceived.

A recent cartoon in *The Oregonian* pits a professional couple against a Gen Yer. The man is expounding, "The job market's tight. We don't want to lose you, so we're increasing your stock options, relaxing the dress code, and installing a cappuccino machine." The Gen Yer wearily responds, "OK, I'll still baby-sit for you." And so it goes, in organizations big and small around the country.

3.

How Not to Manage Generation Y:

The Seven Traits
of the Worst Managers

MARCI, A MANAGER at SubStandard Insurance Company, marched into the open office area of the claims department, a stack of reports in her arms. She ignored the staffers along her heated path to Jim's desk. Her scowl was strictly reserved for its target: Jim.

Jim! Yet another one of those incompetent, lazy interns the company dumped on her every summer. A 19-year-old know-it-all who bristled at her commands; a "Mister Know-Nothing" who wanted to discuss every procedure she required him to follow. Right from the start he galled, suggesting ways to increase efficiency before he'd even been there a week! But why had Marci been surprised? One look at his tee shirt and jeans, and she'd been able to size him up immediately: a "professional" pain in the neck—more of a burden than a help.

And then all those requests that had to be stifled, like Jim wanting to bring in his own desk lamp and family pictures. She'd been ready as ever with her rationale against that: "Listen, kid, you're just here for the summer. If I did it for you, I'd have to do it for all the interns." He could be persistent though, especially about having coffee or lunch together so he could "ask a bunch of questions I've been keeping in a notebook." Well, who had the time for *that?* And he didn't "get" the message at all. When he told her he wanted feedback about what he did right as well as what he did wrong, she said for what felt like the hundredth time, "*Give me a break*. I've told you, this is just an internship."

Now, six weeks into his internship, Jim was delivering just as Marci had expected. She had to keep on his back to get the smallest results, all the while deflecting those endless questions and holding the reins on his irritating enthusiasm. But *this* time! Marci's anger seethed behind her grit teeth as she reached his desk. For a moment she just glared at him.

"Jim, you blew it *again*," she shot out. "I told you to add up the claims figures in each column with a calculator and type them out on a separate sheet in column form so I could insert them in my monthly report."

He looked truly dumbfounded. "But Marci, all you said was 'Add up these numbers.' And there are lots of ways to do that. If you had told me exactly how to do it, I'd have done it that way. But since you didn't, I came up

with my own way. And I think you'll agree that it's a
much better way to do it." His voice went up an eager
notch. "You see, I set up a simple spreadsheet so I can
give you the numbers any way you want. In fact, if you
give me your report, I can just feed the data into the
right column, and—"

"I don't care how you did it!" Marci exploded. "When
I tell you what I want, just do it! *Now redo it the way I
just told you.* And try filing these!" She dumped the stack
of reports on his desk and stormed out. A collective sigh
of relief filled the room. The rest of the staff had escaped
her wrath—at least this time.

"Just because I'm an intern," Jim mumbled, "doesn't
mean I don't know anything." Another intern, Kathy,
approached his desk. "Don't let her get to you. She's like
this with everybody." Across the aisle, Jeff, also an intern,
chimed in, "Yeah, the wicked witch flunked charm school
and Management 101 all in the same year. Forget her."

The three young interns laughed as they compared notes
about their domineering manager and tossed around apt
nicknames for her.

Marci! She was the type of manager who would delegate
small menial chunks of work one day and unreasonable
mountains another. She never defined the big picture or
specific goals, so her commands often seemed vague and

contradictory. She blamed everyone but herself when communication broke down and things didn't get done her way—and her way was always the right way, the only way, to do things. Marci had her command post—and no one was going to undermine it.

The more the interns bantered about the manager, the less humorous her behavior seemed.

"She treats us like grunts," Kathy said. "I'd be in shock if she ever said one nice thing about what we produce."

"I gave up trying to take initiative a long time ago," Jeff confided. "I busted my tail one time on a project she gave me, and then she never even looked at it. Why bother?"

Jim sighed. "And I thought this internship would be an opportunity to learn and contribute. Now I can't wait to get out of here. The best thing I've learned is how *not* to treat people."

* * *

This is a ridiculous scenario, right? What manager could be as bad as Marci? The fact is, she's a composite of the managerial traits Yers complain about most frequently. She's domineering, closed-minded, and unfriendly—even insulting. She's an ineffective delegator with poor communication skills who has little tolerance for innovation and even less insight into what motivates Generation Y.

Certainly, few managers have all these traits; but many managers have at least one. And any can be damaging and demoralizing to young workers.

During our interviews we asked hundreds of Gen Yers to describe their "worst" managers. Those descriptions revealed seven traits that are particularly obnoxious to this generation. Listen to what they say about the Marcis in their lives. Could they say the same about you or your managers?

THE SEVEN TRAITS OF THE WORST MANAGERS

1. Close-Mindedness

— "They Never Listen!"

Remember that Gen Yers grew up with access to a tidal wave of information and the technology to surf it. Thus they're comfortable with multiple points of view and many ways of doing things. Managers who get stuck in the "My way/Highway" paradigm will inevitably butt heads with young workers.

If you've become an "expert" in your field, you especially need to practice open-mindedness. Quite often, experts are tempted to close out other voices, opinions, and perspectives. But if you do that, you'll lose the enthusiasm, creativity, and productivity of your young talent.

Listen to the Voices of Gen Y:

[My boss] wanted everything done a certain way. He would look over your shoulder as you did it, and if you screwed up, he wouldn't like it at all. He wouldn't listen to anything—that was the most frustrating thing. I was doing a lot of basic computer stuff, and he wouldn't listen to anything. There are multiple ways of doing things on the computer, and . . . having grown up with [computers, I often] could do it quicker than the way he was used to. But he would be there looking over my shoulder, making sure things got done his way.

— 20-Year-Old in Early Education

She never listened to any ideas. She never even considered them. She would pooh-pooh [my ideas] because I'm so young; yet her business remained largely unsuccessful.

— 22-Year-Old Bookkeeping Assistant

She was telling everyone in the office what to do, and she wasn't really open. She thought her ideas were always right—[the right way] was always her way to do things. She was closed-minded.

— 20-Year-Old Assistant Accountant
Intern

2. Ineffective Delegation

— *"They Don't Assign Meaningful Work!"*

Gen Yers want to contribute and feel they're adding value to an organization. If what they're doing seems no more than grunt work or busy work, then every day becomes an interminable "Groundhog Day," a déjà vu with no possibility for growth and accomplishment.

These young people want to be sufficiently challenged with the pace and scope of work. Remember, increasing responsibility "lights their fire." If you're not sure you're challenging them enough, simply ask. Gen Yers will be happy to tell you.

Listen to the Voices of Gen Y:

I always had to go and ask for [more work] several times a day. I wish they had given me more responsibility to begin with. I think they weren't sure if I could handle everything—which wasn't a big deal. . . . They would just give everyone really little chunks of things to do.

— 20-Year-Old Public Relations Intern

My manager never gave me work to do, so I felt like I was worthless and wasting company money.

— 20-Year-Old Office Assistant

I work for an insurance company in an extremely boring office. The beginning of the summer was especially boring. All I did was go over files. It was like [being in the film] Groundhog Day. I did the same thing every day. Now that I'm done with that project, there's nothing for me to do. I always ask people what to do, but I get no direction, no guidance. I don't know what I'm doing day to day. It's miserable.

— 21-Year-Old Support Staffer

3. Lack of Knowledge and Organization Skills

— "They Don't Know What They're Doing!"

Gen Yers expect their bosses to know more than they do. To their minds, that's why people have earned the title and position. As a 21-year-old language tutor explained, "You want to look up to your [bosses] and feel that there is something you can learn from them."

Indeed, Gen Yers are forgiving if their managers are less than adept at technology. That's an opportunity for them to shine. But when managers aren't proficient in the core competencies of management—in such areas as organization, planning, decision making, and goal setting—Gen Yers find them lacking in credibility.

Positions and titles mean little to this generation. Rather, the person who has hands-on knowledge and who can help them get the job done and accomplish their goals wins their loyalty and admiration.

Listen to the Voices of Gen Y:

[My boss] was disorganized, insecure, and wishy-washy. I ended up making as many company decisions as she did while I was working for her. I felt more responsible than she did.

> — 20-Year-Old Animal Handler at
> an Entertainment Park

She didn't know what she was doing. I knew more about the place than she did. She just didn't think through the decisions that she was making. Eventually she ended up firing a friend of mine, and I quit because of it. After that, they fired her and got me back. They knew I was more important. It was weird because she was upper management, but she was just dumber than dirt. She really didn't know what was happening.

> — 18-Year-Old Fast-Food Worker

4. Inability to Train or to Facilitate Training

— *"They Don't Know How to Teach!"*

Since ongoing learning is so important to Gen Yers, managers who don't provide effective training or any training earn low marks. Feeling incompetent deflates the Gen Y self-confidence and self-esteem.

Of course, not every manager is a gifted trainer. But the good news is, you don't need to be a trainer yourself. If you can facilitate training, and ensure that Gen Yers get the skills and knowledge they need when they need them, then Gen Yers will be satisfied.

Listen to the Voices of Gen Y:

My worst boss was a lady who never seemed to be doing any work herself. She didn't train any of her employees very well. She told me I was doing a good job, but she seemed to tell everyone that, even [those who were] slackers. I never really felt comfortable talking with her, and if I didn't understand something, I felt nervous about telling her. I felt that she wouldn't be able to show me anyway. She would just give me a paper telling me how to do it.

— 21-Year-Old Public Relations Intern

My worst manager was impatient with me, as I was a little slow at learning how to use the machines [and figuring] out where things were.

— 20-Year-Old Multimedia Assistant

5. Disrespect for Young People

— *"They Treat Us Like Idiots!"*

The "self-esteem generation" bristles when people treat them like know-nothing kids. They believe that what they can do is much more important than how old they are. Their parents, teachers, and counselors have taught them that respect must be earned and that it should be granted when earned.

Keep in mind, Gen Yers have been told all their lives that they "can do anything"; so it's not surprising they dislike being told, "You can't do this because you're just a kid."

Listen to the Voices of Gen Y:

[My employers] were nice people, but they didn't treat me with any type of respect. Didn't assume that I had any sort of abilities. It made me not as enthusiastic about going to work or doing what they asked.

— 21-Year-Old Office Worker at an Investment Firm

*[My boss] was formalistic, harsh, and demanding.
Rather than treat me as a person, he preferred
to address me as a worthless subordinate and
unworthy addition to the workplace.*

> — 22-Year-Old Congressional
> Legislative Intern

*My manager was horrendous. We were not
slackers, we were not lazy, and we were definitely
not incompetent; yet she treated us like all of those
things. I ran a computer lab by myself and taught
kids all day long on computers. I never had one
word of encouragement for all the work that I did
or for all the work that I did that was outside of
my job. She just completely disrespected us and
treated us like idiots.*

> — 19-Year-Old Public School
> Teaching Assistant

*If [the people you work for don't] respect you,
you're not going to respect them. I've noticed that,
being head guard. I have younger people under me.
If I don't respect them, they're not going to respect
me back.*

> — 21-Year-Old Head Lifeguard
> at a Public Pool

6. Intimidating Attitude

— *"Who Wants to Work with Anyone Like This?"*

Like anyone with an ounce of self-respect, the typical Gen Yer doesn't respond well to management by intimidation. Domineering people with short, hot tempers leave this generation cold. Condescending people who yell and scream lose their loyalty instantly.

Remember: Gen Yers have access to highly sophisticated psychological interpretations of abusive behavior—in short form through the media and in detail through on-line medical journals—and they know about lawsuits. Moreover, parents, teachers, and counselors have taught them, from an early age, never to let anyone treat them in a way that makes them feel uncomfortable. Consequently, these young people are not going to sit around and feel victimized. They are going to investigate, gather information, interpret, and respond accordingly.

Listen to the Voices of Gen Y:

> *[My boss] was a nasty, evil old woman who made the already bad working environment worse. She'd yell at people a lot and just generally did not make people want to come to work.*
>
> — 19-Year-Old Telemarketer

He was very domineering—always looking over your shoulder to see if something [was] wrong, and when it [was, he was] very quick to point out it was because of your own stupidity and not an overlooked mistake.

— 22-Year-Old Clerk

She wasn't very nice, and you never knew when she was going to be in a good or bad mood. She would yell at you when you did anything wrong, and she would do it in front of several people.

— 20-Year-Old Restaurant Host

The Golden Rule applies to everyone. And the yelling thing has got to go.

— 21-Year-Old Machinist

7. Overemphasis on Outward Appearance

— *"Are They Managing the Book or the Cover?"*

Dress is a prime generational battleground. From the short skirts of the '20s to the long hair of '60s to the body piercing of the '90s, it has been, and continues to be, a contentious issue. So pick your dress-code battles wisely.

If dress matters, it matters. Dress needs to fit the occasion, your clientele, your work environment, your safety standards. And even if Gen Yers initially try to push the envelope, the most talented among them know that.

If dress doesn't really matter—if you're only trying to impose your fashion sense on others—let it go. You may find that the person under the tattoos, oddly dyed hair, and body piercings is the best person for the job.

For example, a staffer at a prestigious law firm told us about a senior partner who diplomatically tried to handle an attire problem with his 19-year-old mailroom clerk. Cloaking his disapproval in a jocular tone, he approached the clerk with "Justin, your fingernail polish doesn't match your jacket." Undaunted, Justin arrived the next day with a jacket that did match! According to the staffer, today Justin commands a higher salary in his new position as webmaster than most administrators in the firm.

One More Gen Y Voice:

Being the kid I once was, I had a lot of bosses who judged me on my appearance. So I liked to wear black—big deal. That didn't mean I was unable to do my job well. There was one job I had where I was constantly being pulled into the "principal's office" and accused of ridiculous things. I believe it had a lot to do with my choice of clothing. . . . If they couldn't bag me on my clothes, they'd find another reason. A word of advice: Never judge a book by its cover.

— 18-Year-Old Salesclerk

NO MORE JERKS, PLEASE!

In the old dues-paying, climb-the-ladder, golden-hand-cuffs days, organizations could overlook managers like Marci because the Jims, Kathys and Jeffs would have tolerated them. But in today's free agency climate, that's no longer true. The price for keeping and promoting ineffective managers is too high. People of all ages, and particularly younger adults, will leave rather than put up with being treated poorly.

The training director at a world-class research facility has been experiencing the truth of that firsthand. He told us that his organization is consistently losing their newest and youngest employees. When we asked why, he replied wearily, "They're not happy here. They don't feel welcomed. Our managers are jerks. They can't afford to be jerks."

Those are stinging words.

You probably have many knowledgeable, effective managers in your organization—people who understand that management is a commitment to people. They're the ones willing to do the high-maintenance work required to motivate a high-maintenance workforce.

And that's what it's going to take to attract and retain the Gen Y workforce. As a 20-year-old banking intern told us, "Hopefully there is some reason why the person above you is the boss." We hope it's because that person has a real talent for building relationships with people and a real grasp of the skills needed to get the work done. Both are essential: the work and the relationships. Balancing them—getting the best work done because you have created the best relationships with the best people—is the key to management in today's economy.

Finally, keep in mind that you don't have to wonder how your managers are treating the staff. If you don't know whether you have a Marci in your midst, just ask your Gen Y employees. They will certainly tell you.

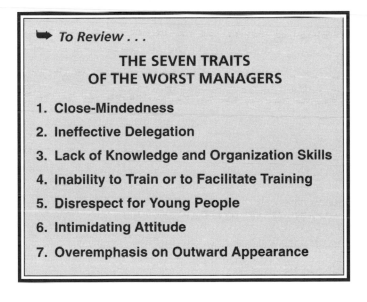

➡ *To Review . . .*

THE SEVEN TRAITS
OF THE WORST MANAGERS

1. **Close-Mindedness**

2. **Ineffective Delegation**

3. **Lack of Knowledge and Organization Skills**

4. **Inability to Train or to Facilitate Training**

5. **Disrespect for Young People**

6. **Intimidating Attitude**

7. **Overemphasis on Outward Appearance**

4.

The Fourteenth Generation's Fourteen Expectations

DON GRABBED A PILE OF ORDER FORMS and headed toward the loading truck on the warehouse floor. The morning strategy meeting had just broken up and he could hear his younger workers buzzing behind him, "No way! What does the big boss think he's doing?"

Don chuckled to himself, pretending he didn't a hear a thing, and climbed into the truck. After studying the purchase order that topped his pile of forms, he aimed the vehicle at the hazardous-products area in the east wing of the 500,000 square-foot facility. He could tell that the already-high temperature of a summer heat wave was climbing even higher.

All morning, Don zipped around the warehouse, trading jibes now and again with the young Gen Y workers, who were still incredulous that the distribution center manager was out there with them and not in his air-conditioned office. His tee shirt and jeans were pretty impressive to them, too, because usually their manager wore casual business attire.

All this was part of Don's plan to deal with an order volume that he'd known would be exceptionally high today. Rather than let his crew drown in the overwhelm, he wanted to make the work fun and challenging. So there he was, honking the truck's horn, asking for the whereabouts of the newest inventory, and trying to meet the time and accuracy standards printed on each order.

Don had tied significant bonuses to the crew's ability to exceed those standards. He also had recently helped redesign the facility's layout and update the motorized equipment, and so workers were well aware of his commitment to help them beat their goals.

That morning, Don stopped only to coach a new worker on forklift maneuvering, to congratulate his newest supervisor on finishing a fantastic project the day before, and to stock up on the filtered water he had ordered delivered to strategic points throughout the area. Since air conditioning was impossible in such a large space, workers were issued sports bottles and encouraged to take time out to keep themselves hydrated during the heat wave.

At lunch Don grabbed a sandwich in the employee cafeteria and traded small talk with a couple of new hires, Kim and Jaime. When he asked how they were doing after two weeks on the job, he got an earful.

"We were talking the other day," Kim said. "If we had hand-held scanners that entered bar codes directly into a computer on our trucks, we could save a whole lot of time double-checking our orders and we'd up our accuracy rates a lot."

"Yeah," Jaime joined in. "Now we're trying to remember what we grabbed from the shelves when we're loading the shipping containers. We got the order form, but, man, sometimes we just get distracted and forget something. If we had that computer in front of us, we could check it and not worry about missing anything."

"Great idea!" Don said, genuinely impressed. "Would you come to Thursday's meeting and present it to the other managers?"

Jaime moved uncomfortably in his seat. "Uh, I don't know, Don. I don't like talking to a bunch of people."

"Me neither," Don laughed. "But if you want to get ahead in any company, it's a great skill to have. Besides, I want the others to know how smart both of you are. Sometimes they don't realize the skills and talents we have out here on the floor."

Kim blushed at the compliment. "Sure we'll do it, Jaime. We can get together and decide what we're going to say."

"OK, then we're set," Don said before Jaime could object. "You're on for 8:15 a.m. in my office on Thursday." He cleaned up his lunch spot and headed back to the warehouse.

"Neat guy," Jaime said after he left. "Nobody ever asked for my ideas before."

Kim agreed. "And nobody ever listened like that. I think this boss is going to be OK."

They followed Don back into the muggy warehouse. And throughout the afternoon, they made sure their horns honked the loudest as their forklifts passed him.

* * *

Few managers are as good as Don. He's a composite of what Gen Yers told us they expect from their managers: a knowledgeable adult who jumps in as a team player when needed, listens to their ideas, recognizes and mentors them, and inspires and motivates them to excel at work.

Yers know intuitively what our research has been telling us for years—and what everyone is saying nowadays: The number one factor affecting employee performance, as well as retention, is the relationship people have with their immediate supervisor. People may be drawn to your business initially because of your name or reputation, but what makes them stay is how well their bosses treat them.

The best managers listen to their employees and care about and support them. They respect and trust, guide and communicate. They challenge, they teach, they give feedback—and they reward. These behaviors are all part of the coaching process.

A 21-year-old who works in the alumni office of a large university spoke for most Gen Y talent when he said:

> I have played sports all my life, so I think I would want to be coached in my job—to have a boss [who] shows and teaches until you understand it, and then gives you the freedom and independence to continue it or expand on it. Gives constructive feedback on a regular basis, but not too often; also encourages and gives positive reward when a job is done right—but doesn't just hand it out for anything.

PUTTING IT ALL TOGETHER: THE FOURTEEN EXPECTATIONS

RainmakerThinking's ongoing research indicates that our fourteenth generation has fourteen expectations which define the way Gen Yers want to be coached by their immediate bosses. These expectations range from providing challenging work that really matters to allowing some flexibility in scheduling to rewarding Yers when they've done a good job. Let's take a closer look.

➡ 1. Provide Challenging Work That Really Matters

One 20-year-old intern at a business magazine told us she was inspired by a manager who

> *always made sure that I knew what I did was really needed and appreciated. So even if it was just Xeroxing, that Xeroxing needed to be done, and I was making a difference by doing it.*

"Just Xeroxing," or stacking inventory, or running lab tests can be given a meaningful context. If managers don't position tasks in the context of larger goals, and if those goals don't challenge Yers' skills and talents, then young workers think, "This is just grunt work. It's a waste of my time." And that's demoralizing.

➡ 2. Balance Clearly Delegated Assignments with Freedom and Flexibility

Gen Yers' confident "I can fend for myself" spirit propels this expectation. They consistently told us they want demanding projects with clear, precise parameters, but also the freedom to do the job their way, at their own pace. As one insightful 16-year-old put it, "I want a manager who is overseeing, not overbearing." Another interviewee, a 21-year-old intern at a government agency, defined the balancing act this way:

> *I'd like my boss to be specific about what needs to get done in the big picture. For example, someone who says, "I need you to make a brochure of what this division does, by next Friday. Come back to me with an idea of how you want to approach it."*

The results are clear; the deadline is set; creativity is encouraged. This works for Yers.

➡ 3. Offer Increasing Responsibility as a Reward for Accomplishments

Buoy Gen Yers' independent spirit through a dose of self-esteem, and you'll drive them to rack up accomplishments. The key here is assigning responsibility.

"I want a lot of responsibilities," says a 21-year-old managing supervisor in the entertainment business. "I want my manager to trust me to handle things and show the confidence that he understands I can get the job done." Another 21-year-old, a server at a national chain restaurant, boasts, "My boss was completely confident in my skills and the way I approached each day at work. He rewarded me by making me a trainer."

To Yers, being assigned more responsibility implies that a manager has trust and confidence in them—a natural boost to their self-esteem.

➥ 4. Spend Time Getting to Know Staff Members and Their Capabilities

Building a successful relationship with Gen Yers is based on knowing them: taking the time to talk about their skills, knowledge, talents, ideas, dreams, aspirations. A 19-year-old receptionist at a university athletic office laid it out this way:

> *When a boss respects your abilities, creativity and independence, the work environment is a lot more pleasant. When someone believes in my abilities, I am more likely to believe in myself. It's encouraging when a manager shows that he or she believes that [the] workforce is competent and able to tackle any challenge.*

Believing your staffers are competent means you know what they can do. This requires "time-outs" for one-on-one coaching sessions, team meetings, informal chats—anything it takes to make a strong connection.

➥ 5. Provide Ongoing Training and Learning Opportunities

Because Gen Yers grew up with interactive media that combined education with fun, they expect learning to be part of their daily lives. They want to experience clear connections between the skills they learn today and the skills they'll use tomorrow.

A 21-year-old advertising intern described her "learn-as-you-go" managers for us:

> *They try to put you in a position where you're not stuck doing things you don't know how to do. They'll sit down and try to explain things —really try [to] help you learn as you do things.*

➡ 6. Establish Mentoring Relationships

"My supervisor at the gym was open to explain[ing] new things," the 20-year-old director of a school hockey program told us. If he didn't understand something, the supervisor would take the time

> *to sit down with me and make sure I understood. But at the same time, he really wanted to get it done the way he showed it to me. He would take as much time as I needed to make sure I understood it. I never thought I was bothering him by asking questions.*

Gen Yers seek out great mentors. Organizations that encourage and support mentoring relationships and provide the time for their people to build these relationships benefit from the increased rapport between managers and their younger workers. Moreover, mentors are afforded the opportunity to make an impact on Gen Yers and give back to the organization.

➡ 7. Create a Comfortable, Low-Stress Environment

For Gen Yers, the primary cause of stress is not the work they're doing but unapproachable managers who yell, make unreasonable demands, or treat them like know-nothing kids. Repeatedly, they told us they appreciate bosses who are "nice," "laid-back," "easygoing," and "not condescending"; in short, managers who make them feel "comfortable."

An 18-year-old college sports publicist told us, "My ideal boss would definitely have to be somebody who makes me feel comfortable." No matter what the job, this boss would be able to provide criticism constructively, in such a way "that it's not like a put-down." But, the publicist added, "I think the biggest thing . . . is that I have to be comfortable. [The boss] can't be a tyrant."

➡ 8. Allow Some Flexibility in Scheduling

There are two possible approaches to the flexibility issue:

- Let people work whenever they want.

- Allow enough give and take to accommodate workers' unexpected scheduling needs (remember that many Gen Yers are still in school, as part-time or full-time students).

Of course, the second approach is the one that most managers can accept more readily.

Flexibility in hours, as well as in projects, assignments, and locations, goes a long way with Gen Yers. For instance, one 20-year-old restaurant hostess spoke highly of a boss who knows that school is her "first priority" and so adjusts her schedule accordingly.

➡ 9. Focus on Work, but Be Personable and Have a Sense of Humor

It's refreshing to discover that most Gen Yers don't want an all-fun, no-work environment. In fact, they are impatient with managers who offer that kind of atmosphere. They want their managers to be serious about the work, but also to have a sense of humor that creates an upbeat atmosphere.

A 20-year-old who works in a university sports office described the balance her boss maintains:

He's just funny, and we just joke around. I know that he feels like my boss, but at the same time it's very low key and I'm not intimidated by him. It helps in my job now that he is not very serious with me. . . . [He will] correct me on things, but it's not like he yells, "You're doing something wrong!" It helps to have a good relationship [with your boss], because if you don't have a good relationship, you won't be happy where you are.

One formula for that relationship is clear: Lighten up *and* demand quality work.

➡10. Balance the Roles of "Boss" and and "Team Player"

Gen Yers want managers who are strong enough to take charge, know enough to provide guidance and leadership, and serve as impressive authority figures. But for Gen Y, the very best managers walk the line between that role and the role of a contributing worker unafraid to get into the trenches with everybody else.

The manager of a 20-year-old animal handler at an entertainment park was an expert at this balancing act. As the Gen Yer explained:

My manager was poised and intelligent. Well informed. She knew more about the company, animals, new goings-on in the world than any of her team members. She never lost her composure, but she was always a team member before being a manager.

To clarify: I never witnessed her in any unprofessional manner, yet I was not intimidated by her, nor did I feel less important than her. She did my job, was great at it. She just happened to be in charge too.

By the same token, though, you always knew who was in charge—she was not bullied or charmed by her team members. Perhaps the central focus here is balance. She knew when to be "one of the team," but she was also an excellent leader.

→11. Treat Yers as Colleagues, Not as Interns or "Teenagers"

One 21-year-old intern in an asset management firm happily reported:

I've never been treated as an intern—it's always been "This is my co-worker, this is my colleague." It's a very small group that we work with. I'm in on everything. Every meeting, every e-mail. Obviously [my co-workers] are very busy and they travel a lot because they are way above me. But that has never made me feel uncomfortable. They set up meetings for me to meet with different directors of different divisions—people that they probably don't get to see on a day-to-day basis.

A baby-boomer manager who understands the power of words told us he's asked his Xers and Yers not to introduce him as their manager when they're out in business situations. He prefers to be positioned as their colleague or associate so that all of them receive equal attention and treatment. Not a bad idea. Out with the terms "manager," "superior," "supervisor." In with "coach," "team leader," "colleague," "associate."

➡ 12. Be Respectful, and Call Forth Respect in Return

Gen Yers don't base their respect for authority figures on mere titles. They respect those who are confident and knowledgeable, who care about them, and who understand the importance of mutual respect. Yers know that the only way you call forth genuine respect is by giving it.

For managers, this means reciprocating the respect that Gen Yers give you. It also means treating Gen Yers with basic respect to begin with, rather than prejudging them and immediately discounting their value. Consider the successful approach used by those folks at the asset management firm cited above.

A 20-year-old retail clerk nailed this issue:

> *Having a great boss like her makes you just not want to do a bad job. . . . When there's that mutual respect, it's more like you do [a good job] not because you have to but because you want to please your boss and you want to do your job well.*

➥ 13. Consistently Provide Constructive Feedback

Gen Yers are emphatic about wanting feedback from their managers. Some said they want "a lot"; others, a "moderate" amount. One 20-year-old simply stated: "As far as feedback [goes], I want whatever is needed."

Why is feedback so important? "I don't like to be lost out there," explained a 21-year-old who works on special projects for a large brokerage firm. "Bosses need to communicate well—tell you what you're doing wrong and communicate exactly what you're supposed to be doing."

What is coaching but an ongoing series of responses to performance? Watch a Little League coach teaching a youngster to slide into third base without injury. Or a drama coach refining the nuances of an actor's speech. Or a consultant helping a small-business owner define her mission. What they all have in common is their ability to respond in ways that facilitate desired results. They don't go out and slide into third base themselves. Or take the actor's place on stage. Or hand the business owner a predetermined mission. Rather, they focus on the strengths and talents of the individual and guide him or her to a successful outcome.

➡ 14. Reward Yers When They've Done a Good Job

One 19-year-old public-school teaching assistant found her supervisor "incredible" because he

> *was always quick with the compliment and letting you know that you were doing a great job. I found his encouragement and recognition made the work atmosphere more comfortable for me.*

In today's competitive work environment, consistent verbal recognition is not enough. Managers must also explore how to customize rewards and incentives to keep their best contributors engaged and on board. When your competitor is offering flextime, tuition reimbursement, and laptop computers to let people know they've done a good job, you must consider recognition beyond words.

A V.A. Hospital administrator gave us a good example of how her organization pulls this off. She told us she has the authority to award a $100 bonus when her people achieve results above and beyond expectations. Moreover, employees have the check in hand a mere 24 hours after producing such results.

When Yers see a clear connection between what they produce and how they are rewarded—and how you've given them a say in making that connection—you are in a much better position to engage their creativity and energy.

➡ *To Review . . .*

THE FOURTEEN EXPECTATIONS OF GENERATION Y

1. Provide challenging work that really matters

2. Balance clearly delegated assignments with freedom and flexibility

3. Offer increasing responsibility as a reward for accomplishments

4. Spend time getting to know staff members and their capabilities

5. Provide ongoing training and learning opportunities

6. Establish mentoring relationships

7. Create a comfortable, low-stress environment

8. Allow some flexibility in scheduling

9. Focus on work, but be personable and have a sense of humor

10. Balance the roles of "boss" and "team player"

11. Treat Yers as colleagues, not as interns or "teenagers"

12. Be respectful, and call forth respect in return

13. Consistently provide constructive feedback

14. Reward Yers when they've done a good job

5.

Best Practices to Meet the Fourteen Expectations

IT'S GOOD TO KNOW what your Gen Y employees expect. But how are you going to meet those expectations so you can maximize your emerging workforce? From our work with hundreds of different organizations we've learned that every organization has its own constraints and its own unique opportunities. Every employer is defined by the organizaton's work as well as its physical location, workplace conditions, scheduling concerns, corporate culture, and, of course, people. Focus on the opportunities rather than the constraints.

In this chapter, we suggest best practices for meeting all fourteen of the Gen Y expectations discussed previously in Chapter 4. Which best practices will work best for you and your managers in your organization? Only you can answer that. But if you implement just a handful of these recommendations, you will be at least one step closer to the strategic advantage of getting the best work out of the best of Generation Y.

The Expectations and Best Practices

Meeting Expectation 1

Provide Challenging Work That Really Matters

- Educate your young workforce not only about the contributions your products and services make to society, but also about how your organization supports its local community.

  Does the organization offer employees paid time off to do volunteer work? Does it make financial contributions to local charities? How is it supporting the environment through programs like recycling and pollution control?

- Ensure that young workers know *why* they are doing whatever it is they are doing.

  Where does the task fit into the "big picture" or a specific goal? Even the smallest job can be positioned as contributing to a larger result. If it can't, it appears meaningless. Why are you asking people to do it?

- Offer team members opportunities to be problem-solvers and innovators by asking them at every team meeting:
  — What are we doing well?
  — What are we doing not so well?
  — How can we do this better?

Remember, Gen Yers are not merely outside-the-box thinkers; they're over-the-wall doers. Create an environment where innovations are encouraged and Gen Yers feel heard.

- Throw "creativity parties" where people can socialize, have fun, and brainstorm a problem the team or the organization is facing.

  Send out an agenda ahead of time stating the issue to be discussed. Then facilitate a brainstorming session, recording everyone's input. Be sure to report back on the outcome of the session: what you're implementing, what you're shelving for future consideration, and what you're deep-sixing.

  Getting people to think and to create together while they're having fun is a potent catalyst for Gen Y productivity.

- Give young people who earn it the opportunity to take on more challenging roles, such as line supervisor, project leader, ad hoc committee chair, and liaison between managers and employees. In today's flattened workplace, the battle cry is "Everyone is a leader!" Tap into Gen Yers' desire for challenge by teaching them leadership skills and engaging them in leadership roles.

- "Rent a techie." Engage your techno-savvy Gen Yers in training computer-challenged employees throughout the organization. And challenge them to help you pursue technological solutions to everyday problems. For example, if people are complaining about boring, unchallenging work, ask Gen Yers to figure out ways to streamline or automate those tasks.

- Ask your Gen Yers to complete the questionnaire on the following page; then use their responses as a springboard to make the changes needed for meeting this expectation consistently.

Meeting Expectation 2

Balance Clearly Delegated Assignments with Freedom and Flexibility

- Create teams focused on well-defined goals, and ensure every member's role is clear. Gen Yers want the assurance that what they're being asked to do will have impact—that it will meet immediate needs and produce concrete results quickly. Your job is to communicate the big picture, the results desired, and what roles those on the team will play in working toward those results.

- Document the results, parameters, deadlines, and results-owners for each task you delegate. Spell out *everything*. Write it down. Make sure contributors each have a copy of the document so they keep their commitments clear.

Questionnaire 1

• FEEDBACK • FEEDBACK • FEEDBACK •

Please answer the questions below and let us know how you feel about these issues. We value your input!

1. Do you feel you are contributing something important by working for our organization? If no, what can we do to make your experience a "yes"? If yes, give us some examples of what is most meaningful to you.

2. Do you feel we are a team of innovative professionals with whom you are proud to be associated? If no, what can we do to make your experience a "yes"? If yes, give us some examples of what is most meaningful to you.

3. Do you think your knowledge, talents, and skills are being used appropriately? If no, what can we do to make your experience a "yes"? If yes, give us some examples of how we do this best.

Don't ask Gen Yers—or any staffer, for that matter—to rely solely on memory when work is assigned. The "in one ear and out the other" phenomenon is alive and well, especially in fast-paced environments, where lots of work has to get done fast.

- Obtain commitment for each result. Ask each results-owner to commit—either verbally or in writing—to taking 100 percent responsibility for his or her assigned tasks. This may sound too formal, but doing it adds a tone of importance to the delegation as well as to the person accepting it.

- Train team members to keep in mind not only their own accountabilities but also . . .

  — the commitments made by others,

  — the deadline constraints each is under,

  — how the timely completion of their work has an impact on the work of others,

  — how their tangible results fit into the overall picture.

Since Gen Yers want to work with committed team players, train them to be responsible players themselves.

- Teach Yers to become time-management experts. This overly structured cohort can't wait to manage their time at work, but they have little experience doing so. Remember: The point is to get them up to speed, and meeting deadlines consistently, so no one has to manage their time for them.

Coach them:

— Teach them how to break up larger results into manageable pieces.

— Help them determine how long tasks take in your department. Base time estimates on your own experience (remembering what it was like when you first tackled the job) or on that of a recent task holder.

— Teach Gen Yers how to build time cushions—the extra hours or days they might need to meet a deadline.

Share your "war stories" about the work-life vagaries that can impede meeting deadlines. You're in the best position to give them a reality check on all the things that can sabotage a final deadline.

• Become an aggressive listener who acknowledges what Yers have to say about how to achieve goals. Their attitude is "You're a smart person with the information and expertise I need. You have great ideas, and I have some too. We need to talk."

Make it clear that you are available as a resource, but, basically, get out of the way and let them work.

- Require all managers to master the skill of delegation:

  — Quickly define purpose and goals.

  — Determine who has 100 percent responsibility for each result, and make that responsibility clear.

  — Define parameters and timetables.

  — Offer results-owners the flexibility to take risks and try new things.

Meeting Expectation 3

Offer Increasing Responsibility as a Reward for Accomplishments

Give Gen Yers responsibility for seizing opportunities for more responsibility. Ask them to complete the feedback questionnaire on the next page, and repeat the process quarterly. Both you and they will have a track record of how effectively they're expanding their skill and knowledge base and adding value in return. And you'll have a clear idea of what new areas they want to pursue. Look for opportunities to use those as performance rewards.

That said, don't forget that too much of a good thing isn't a good thing. Too much responsibility placed on shoulders not ready to bear it can be just as demotivating as too little responsibility. As a 16-year old retail store employee put it, "Don't throw me the keys to the store until you make sure I'm comfortable enough to catch them."

Questionnaire 2

• FEEDBACK • FEEDBACK • FEEDBACK •

*Please tell me about your work experience in the past **three** months, and what you project for the future.*

1. What skills, knowledge, and proof of value have you gained?

2. What tasks or assignments are you doing better today than you were three months ago? Explain.

3. What new tasks, responsibilities, and projects have you tackled?

4. What mentorship opportunities have you pursued?

5. How have you made this organization a better place?

6. How has this organization made you a better person?

7. What new responsibilities would you like to pursue in the *next* three months?

8. How can I help you prepare for those responsibilities? For example, would training or mentorship help you?

Meeting Expectation 4

Spend Time Getting to Know Staff Members and Their Capabilities

- Capitalize on informal "getting to know you," time-out times. Get ready for spontaneous brainstorming or coaching sessions, in the cafeteria or some other accommodating space.

  Your most productive relationship-building times with Yers may well be outside the office or cubicle. So go for a walk. Take them to lunch. Stop for a chat in the break room. Look for opportunities to listen—and seize them.

- Encourage staff members to talk about what's important to them, what's on their minds—music, family, hobbies, friends, anything. You'll gain a lot of insight into what makes them tick.

- Plan one-to-one meetings on a consistent basis (weekly or at least biweekly).

  The purpose of these meetings is simple: to head problems off at the pass. In addition to showing that you take a genuine interest in them and their work, you'll also uncover questions and concerns you could easily overlook.

  A sample agenda is shown on the following page.

• SAMPLE AGENDA •

Manager:
Employee: Date:

■ Updates on current tasks, responsibilities, projects:

■ Difficulties or frustrations you're experiencing:

■ Where you want to be and what you want to be working
  on within the next three months:

■ What it would take to get you there in terms of training,
  mentorship, and so on:

■ Your recommendations for making your job less
  stressful and more satisfying:

Follow-up actions must be taken by this date:
Date for next meeting:

- Encourage Gen Yers to create and maintain an achievement file/career portfolio. Contents should include:

  — Training they've completed

  — Goals they've achieved

  — New ideas they've suggested and/or implemented

  — Letters or notes of praise from customers, co-workers, and managers

  — Any other indication of how they add value to your organization

This is not only a great morale booster for them, but a useful tool for you. When the time comes for performance evaluations, simply borrow their portfolio. It will provide you with a wealth of information about their contributions and successes, some of which you may have forgotten.

Meeting Expectation 5

Provide Ongoing Training and Learning Opportunities

- Clearly define the skills and knowledge that employees must learn in order to advance to the next project or level. Create a road map of ongoing learning opportunities that will keep your young workforce engaged. Once training opportunities dry up, so does Gen Y enthusiasm.

- Carefully develop customized learning plans to teach those skills "just in time." Like older adults, Yers learn best when they know they're going to use the learning immediately. "What's going to be on the test?" is one of their favorite questions. That's why training them for the short haul—for the next task, the next assignment—makes sense.

  One size doesn't fit all, especially when it comes to training. The old notion that you wait to offer a training session until there's a "class" to be trained simply doesn't work. And it's counterproductive. You hold contributors back from contributing, and demotivate them in the process.

- Keep in your database up-to-date inventories of the marketable knowledge and skills your employees have mastered. This is the foundation for a talent pool of workers you can tap for project teams, ad hoc committees, and special focus groups.

- Design focused assignments to keep Yers up to date on the latest news and trends in your industry. Have them share their research at staff meetings. Techno-savvy Yers will have little difficulty with this kind of assignment and can "show off" their research skills.

- Keep alive the energy, excitement, and enthusiasm for learning by encouraging Gen Yers to anticipate their own training needs. By tapping into their need for freedom and independence, you not only empower them to learn consistently, but also give them owner-ship of their training process. Encourage them to identify the tasks they want to learn next, and to sell themselves to project leaders to get those assignments.

- Be sure to provide state-of-the-art, multimedia training resources that are easily accessible to every employee. Remember that the digital generation expects speed, customization, interactivity, and fun.

  Do you offer a variety of resources to match Gen Y's diverse learning styles? For instance, CD-ROMs, audiotapes, and videocassettes; books, articles, and research tools; knowledgeable professionals, sample documents, and databases; public workshops and onsite classroom training.

- Periodically test employees to monitor the effective-ness of your training and the depth of their learning. Who's getting it, and who's not? Who needs more instruction?

- Have employees apply what they're learning as soon as possible—maybe first in trial runs and role playing and then "for real." Gen Yers are practical learners. They want to know immediately "What can I do with what I now know?"

- Train your trainers to be facilitators who understand that Yers are wired for the speed, customization, and interactivity of technology, and that they appreciate fun, entertaining teaching styles that quickly engage them.

- Dedicate sufficient time to learning activities. Time is the most overlooked resource. If you value training, you must allocate adequate time for it.

- Make everyone a teacher. A teacher is someone who is further along the path, the person who knows more than you do. Some people on your team will already be expert time-managers. Make them your time-management teachers. Some will be expert at conflict resolution. Make them your conflict-resolution teachers. Some will be great at written communication, some at oral communication, some at customer service. Find the stars in your midst and tap their talents so everyone benefits.

  Ask your star players to share the "secrets" of their success—their best practices, tips, strategies, hints. Create an informal handbook of the best suggestions and pass it along to new hires. Gen Yers respond well to people who have "been through it"—people who can help them get up to speed quickly and easily.

- Throw onsite or offsite learning parties where people can help one another improve their technical prowess, communication skills, deal-making abilities, and so on. Focus on one skill area at a time and engage your "stars" to head up these informal but informative events.

- Broadcast failures (lightheartedly, of course) so everyone can learn from them. With managers leading the way, create a "we learn from our mistakes" environment. "I blew it big time. I won't do that again!" is the spirit.

Some organizations even give out weekly awards to employees who have made the biggest mistakes but learned important lessons from them.

Meeting Expectation 6

Establish Mentoring Relationships

- Create a network of mentors—people within your organization who are star players and who are willing to pass their strategies and skills along to Gen Yers. Make a list of those mentors, including areas of expertise, and keep it in your database for easy access. Encourage Yers to seek out those individuals for informal chats, brainstorming sessions, or training opportunities.

- Promote mentor/mentee events like ice-cream socials, brown-bag lunches, workshops on communication skills, and the like. These are opportunities for employees in mentor relationships to come together to celebrate, to learn, to have fun.

- Recognize mentors. Take a tip from the training center of a prestigious research facility, and hang a mentoring board in a prominent place. The center's board displays pictures of people who mentor college interns and personal assessments of their experiences. What is striking is how many of those mentors report they get as much out of mentoring as the students, if not more. For instance, one scientist was able to spend more time than usual doing research and "found [the students] very capable and eager to work in the lab and to learn how research is conducted. The enthusiasm of the students is contagious, and working together was just plain fun."

- Reward Yers by taking them to important meetings so they can meet people who have succeeded in the careers that interest them. Rubbing elbows with stars outside your department or organization is another sure-fire Gen Yer motivator.

Meeting Expectation 7

Create a Comfortable, Low-Stress Environment

- Create a "caring comfort zone." Gen Yers want to know that you care about them as people. Find the time to talk with Gen Yers about what interests them beyond work. They don't want you to be a best friend—quite the contrary. They want you to be the knowledgeable adult in charge. But they're looking for those who will strike a balance between getting to know them personally and maintaining a good working relationship.

A 19-year-old banquet server put it very simply: "I want to work with someone [I can] talk to about regular things going on in my life, and they care." Like Xers, Yers are not loyal to organizations. They're loyal to people. And genuine caring creates genuine loyalty.

- Create an "emotional comfort zone." A 20-year-old intern at an international bank describes her ideal manager in these terms:

  A good boss would be very big on the open-door policy, not condescending, good at explaining things. I would want my boss to be really laid-back, or at least laid-back enough that I could talk to them easily and ask them questions.

  A 19-year-old member of an engineering survey crew used this coaching analogy:

  If a coach is always yelling at you or telling you the things you're doing wrong, then you become very conscious of the way that you're playing. Then you start worrying about being taken out or . . . being fired. And I think you can't perform with the [necessary] confidence.

Ask yourself:

— What emotional impact do I have on my young workers?

— How do I want them to feel when they walk away from me each day?

— Am I diminishing their confidence, or enhancing it?

— Do they feel secure enough to ask me questions or unafraid to talk to me about anything?

- Create a "physical comfort zone." As long as Gen Yers achieve their goals consistently, managers should encourage them to "own" their work area.

  — Let them arrange their desk and chair however they like.

  — Permit them to listen to CDs or the radio at a volume that does not distract others.

  — Allow them to surround themselves with appropriate pictures, clippings, images they enjoy.

  — Encourage them to take stretch breaks, "power naps," a day off, or a vacation when they need it.

- Try out the following exercise for creating a comfortable, low-stress environment.

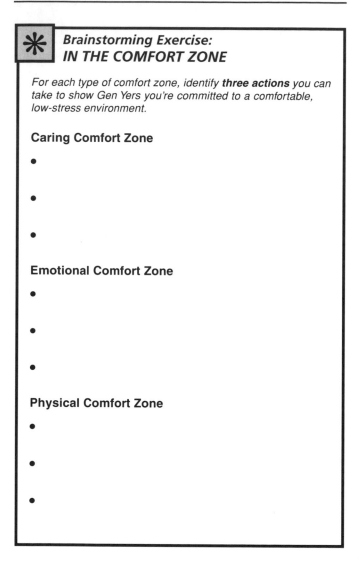

✳ *Brainstorming Exercise:*
IN THE COMFORT ZONE

*For each type of comfort zone, identify **three actions** you can take to show Gen Yers you're committed to a comfortable, low-stress environment.*

Caring Comfort Zone

•

•

•

Emotional Comfort Zone

•

•

•

Physical Comfort Zone

•

•

•

Meeting Expectation 8

Allow Some Flexibility in Scheduling

- Take an inventory of all the tasks and responsibilities assigned to a particular Gen Yer. Then decide which ones need to be done in a certain place at specific hours, and which ones don't. Use those that don't as opportunities to lend more flexibility to the job. Then position that flexibility as a reward for good performance.

- Set standards for requests for time off or schedule changes. If your work situation simply requires that someone be in a certain place at a certain time, empower your staffers to collaborate on covering bases when one of them needs time off or a change in schedule. Instead of trying to juggle the workload to please everyone, allow staffers to figure out the logistics. Let them know that, at a minimum, they should agree on the following:

  — **Timing:** How long before the desired day off or schedule change (barring emergencies, of course) must a request be made?

  — **Coverage:** What's the process for getting someone to cover their responsibilities?

You know they have personal lives, and you want to be flexible, but flexibility doesn't mean irresponsibility. The work still has to get done. However, giving your staffers ownership of the process makes it both easier for you and more efficient for them.

- Get rid of "sick time" and transform it into personal time off or customized time off.

Personal Time Off: The old paradigm of sick days was indeed sick. People had to lie to take care of personal business or to decompress after a stressful schedule. That's why many organizations have switched to the more user-friendly PTO. Allocate a specific number of personal days—these may cover holidays, vacations, personal business days, bona fide sick days, stress-relief days—and encourage people to use them whenever needed. Consider allowing "personal hours off" too, for when workers just want to leave an hour or two earlier or come in later.

Customized Time Off: If you really want to be on the cutting edge, discard PTO too. Give those who beat deadlines and exceed goals the privilege of customizing their time off. Of course, this means you have to move from managing the clock to coaching for results, and that is a dramatic shift in management perspective. But it's the only way to manage a flexible, fluid workforce in an ever-changing marketplace and to provide the flexibility every generation seeks.

- Use the next exercise to brainstorm ways to increase flexibility.

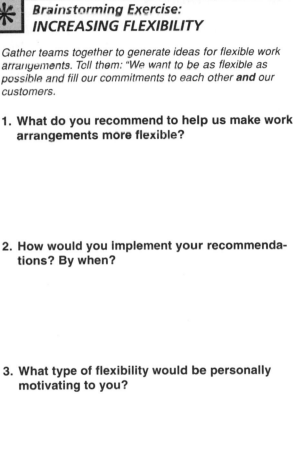

Brainstorming Exercise:
INCREASING FLEXIBILITY

Gather teams together to generate ideas for flexible work arrangements. Tell them: "We want to be as flexible as possible and fill our commitments to each other **and** our customers.

1. **What do you recommend to help us make work arrangements more flexible?**

2. **How would you implement your recommendations? By when?**

3. **What type of flexibility would be personally motivating to you?**

Meeting Expectation 9

Focus on Work, but Be Personable and Have a Sense of Humor

- Concentrate, first and foremost, on the work to be done, but do so in a lighthearted manner. You can be serious about the work without taking yourself too seriously.

- Help Gen Yers find the fun in work, such as learning new skills, building relationships with impressive people, and achieving tangible results they can put their name on. You don't need video-game breaks or practical jokes to make work fun.

- Create a "fun budget" and administer it. Something as simple as lunches together or "bagel Mondays" or "ice-cream Wednesdays" can create a feeling of camaraderie. Group trips, chair massages, or after-noon sports breaks take the culture of fun one step further.

  Just be careful: What is fun for some people can be a burden for others.

- Lighten up and monitor your own stress level. Make sure you're taking care of yourself—physically, mentally, emotionally, spiritually. Remember one of Gen Yers' most commonly used terms for a good boss: "laid-back."

Meeting Expectation 10

Balance the Roles of "Boss" and "Team Player"

- Look for opportunities to get out of your office, roll up your sleeves, and work side by side with your Gen Yers.

  Maverick CEO Herb Kelleher of Southwest Airlines requires his managers to play baggage handler, reservation clerk, or ticket agent once a month. They stay in touch with the challenges their people experience every day as well as learn the art of team playership.

- Pass the leadership hat around. In a fluid workplace, there are many opportunities to share leadership roles. Search for opportunities to let your Gen Yers run a project with you as team player. Here's a chance to role-model what good playership is all about.

- Recognize that the best team leaders are the best team players. How effective are you—and all the members of your team, for that matter—with the essential skills of playership?

  To find out, complete the following evaluation tool "How Well Are We Working Together?" Have team members complete it too. Then brainstorm ways to improve everyone's behaviors, using the brainstorming exercise that follows the evaluation tool.

• TEAM MEMBERSHIP EVALUATION •
How Well Are We Working Together?

Directions: Listed below are some essential behaviors of team playership. Focus on the people you work closely with every day, including your manager; then check off how often the listed behaviors actually occur as you relate to those people.

As a member of this team, I . . .	Always	Often	Sometimes	Rarely	Never
Understand our goals and am committed to accomplishing them.	❏	❏	❏	❏	❏
Work in an organized, systematic way that facilitates results.	❏	❏	❏	❏	❏
Am concerned about and interested in the success and well-being of other members.	❏	❏	❏	❏	❏
Trust each member to fulfill commitments.	❏	❏	❏	❏	❏
Listen and respond with openness and empathy.	❏	❏	❏	❏	❏
Help to create a flexible, "fun" environment.	❏	❏	❏	❏	❏
Acknowledge and celebrate diversity.	❏	❏	❏	❏	❏
Share thoughts, feelings, rationales.	❏	❏	❏	❏	❏

TEAM MEMBERSHIP EVALUATION (concluded)					
As a member of this team, I . . .	Always	Often	Sometimes	Rarely	Never
Create procedures that make the workflow as easy as possible.	☐	☐	☐	☐	☐
Understand the stressors in each team member's job.	☐	☐	☐	☐	☐
Provide other members with helpful suggestions when they ask for them.	☐	☐	☐	☐	☐
Seek constructive feedback from others.	☐	☐	☐	☐	☐
Recognize star performers on the team.	☐	☐	☐	☐	☐
Have developed a "learning attitude" toward mistakes.	☐	☐	☐	☐	☐
Embrace cooperation rather than competition as a learning value.	☐	☐	☐	☐	☐

> **Now ask your team to do the "Working Better Together" brainstorming exercise on the following page.**

Brainstorming Exercise:
WORKING BETTER TOGETHER

• STEP A

Gather your team members together, and come to a consensus on *three behaviors* that you all want to improve.

Behavior 1:

Behavior 2:

Behavior 3:

• STEP B

For each of the three behaviors, brainstorm:

How can we make this behavior more productive for our team?

Behavior 1:

Behavior 2:

Behavior 3:

Meeting Expectation 11

Treat Yers as Colleagues, Not as Interns or "Teenagers"

- Seek Gen Yer input on decisions, minor or major, that have a direct impact on their work. Make it clear that their spontaneous input is welcome anytime.

- Have Yers represent you at meetings or workshops when you can't attend. Prime them for what they can expect and for what information you want upon their return.

- Place a high value on their innovative spirit. If you only hire people who think like you, what you have is a lot of redundancy on your staff. You need people who can push the envelope, who can act as well as think over the brick-and-mortar walls.

  Gen Yers are eager to find new ways of doing things. Do you encourage and recognize their innovative ideas?

- Be aware that language is important. Using terms like "subordinate," "underling," and "second-tier worker" does little to enhance self-esteem. If you want the best young talent to work professionally, you need to address them as professionals. Consider "loading-dock specialist," "inventory technician," and "hospitality professional."

Sound silly? Not really. Words encapsulate values, attitudes, and energy. Challenge young people to grow into professional roles by giving them professional designations.

- Ask your Gen Yers to complete the following feedback questionnaire; then discuss their answers and suggestions at your next one-on-one meeting.

Meeting Expectation 12

Be Respectful, and Call Forth Respect in Return

- When dealing with Gen Y employees, choose your words and actions as carefully as you would with other co-workers.

- When assigning, collaborating, or evaluating work, focus (in your own mind) on the value your Gen Yers are adding to the end result. If they are not adding enough value, take responsibility for that management failure and address the problem squarely. What do you need to do as a manager to make sure the young talent on your team is adding value?

- Remind yourself, as often as necessary, just why you are utilizing Gen Y talent in your organization, on your team, or for a particular project.

- Conduct an honest self-evaluation of your relationship with your Gen Yers, and ask all your managers

Questionnaire 3

• FEEDBACK • FEEDBACK • FEEDBACK •

Please answer the questions below and let me know what you think about my management style. I value your input!

1. Do I seek your input on decisions that affect you? If no, share an example of an opportunity I missed. If yes, share an example of when and how I did that.

2. What opportunities to attend meetings and workshops as my representative have you found beneficial? What opportunities would you like in the future?

3. Do I encourage you to be an innovator? If no, share an example of an opportunity I missed. If yes, share an example of when and how I did that.

---

to do the same. Ask yourself questions such as:

— Are my Gen Yers comfortable with me?

— Can they trust me to listen?

— Do they find me flexible and open to their ideas?

— Am I fun to work with while holding them to a high standard?

— Do I balance the roles of boss and team player?

— Do I treat Gen Yers as colleagues, or as underlings?

- Draft a "Declaration of Respect" with your staffers (see sample on facing page). When you come to a consensus, post your declaration where everyone can see it and use it as a guideline for daily interactions.

Meeting Expectation 13

Consistently Provide Constructive Feedback

- Look for key opportunities to coach your employees. Mistakes, questions, completed assignments, and difficult customer interactions are all opportunities to get your Gen Yers back on track and keep them there. Opportunities may vary from day to day and person to person, but they appear all the time. Seize the ones that will have the greatest impact on your Yers' work.

- Follow the FAST Feedback™ model, engaging your people in a management relationship defined by on-going responsive communication. "FAST" stands for:

• SAMPLE DECLARATION OF RESPECT •

We will strive to be straightforward in our dealings with each other.

We will listen carefully and give each other support when we need it.

We will treat each other with respect, even when we disagree.

We will give people credit for their ideas, and not claim them as our own.

We will challenge each other to achieve excellence, and not allow ourselves to get stuck in mediocrity.

We will keep our promises, and if we can't, we will explain why.

We will take responsibility for our own behavior, and not for each other's.

We will do everything in our power to help each other succeed.

Frequent—Tune in to each person's needs and style. Everyone has a unique "frequency."

Accurate—Check your facts and say only what you are certain is true.

Specific—Always tell people exactly what you want them to do next.

Timely—Give feedback regularly and as soon as possible after the performance in question.

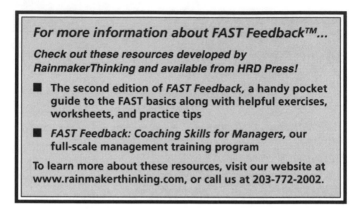

- Remember that great coaching requires zooming in on what people did right, what they did wrong, and what they must do next to get back on course—to continue improving and growing.

- Focus on one issue at a time.

- Slow down the conversation. Take time to gather information. Invite your staffer to suggest how to do things right the next time. Be prepared to offer strategies that work. All of these elements are important if you're going to get the results you want.

- Avoid losing your cool. Take a few deep breaths before meeting with any staffer who has blown it. Close your door and pound on a pillow if you have to. Do anything but yell or scream at employees. Intimidation makes people of all ages look for exit signs.

Meeting Expectation 14

Reward Yers When They've Done a Good Job

- Base your incentives and rewards on one factor and one factor only: *performance.* Establish clear performance guidelines for every employee, and monitor performance closely and fairly. Then reward people when they perform, and don't reward them when they don't perform.

- Determine which tasks, projects, and responsibilities are suitable for short-term incentives. What must someone get done, by when, and up to what standards to earn an incentive?

- Ask each Gen Yer to list the incentives that mean the most to him or her. Discuss the list during your next one-on-one meeting, afternoon stroll, or lunchtime chat. Determine which goals, tasks, and responsibilities would earn each incentive. Have this discussion on an ongoing basis so you're both on the same page when it comes to this "pay for performance" issue.

- Deliver rewards when people *deliver results,* no sooner and no later. Timely delivery is one key to the success of this rewards system. Yers love the immediacy of "I did this; I got that." If you don't deliver, you've taken a step backwards.

In Conclusion . . .

GENERATION Y PRESENTS the next gigantic opportunity and the next considerable challenge for managers and business leaders in the new economy. As we have seen, Gen Yers are upbeat and full of self-esteem. They think education is cool, and they are paving the way to a more open, tolerant society. They also are volunteering more of their time to good causes than perhaps any generation in history.

These "global citizens born in the late seventies and early eighties" (GCBLSEEs) are determined to do meaningful work that makes a difference. They want to work with great teams of committed, high-quality people. They expect to work hard and to succeed beyond the wildest dreams of those who wish the best for them. They know already the kinds of bosses they dislike and the kinds that bring out the very best in them. They know how they want to be managed, and they won't accept it any other way.

Aided by new technologies and more effective organizations, Generation Y may add more value in the workplace than any generation in history. They may also be the most demanding generation in history. Ready or not, here they come. *Are you ready?*

Recommended Resources

Barna, George. *Baby Busters: Disillusioned Generation.* Chicago: Northfield Pub, 1994.

Barna, George. *Generation Next: What You Need to Know About Today's Youth.* Ventura, CA: Regal Books, 1997.

Epstein, Jonathan S., ed. *Youth Culture: Identity in a Postmodern World.* Oxford: Blackwell Publishers, 1998.

Giroux, Henry A. *Stealing Innocence: Youth, Corporate Power and the Politics of Culture.* New York: St. Martin's Press, Inc., 2000.

Hersch, Patricia. *A Tribe Apart: A Journey into the Heart of American Adolescence.* New York: Ballantine Books, 1999.

Hicks, Kathy, and Rick Hicks. *Boomers, Xers, and Other Strangers.* Wheaton, IL: Tyndale House, 1999.

Hine, Thomas. *The Rise and Fall of the American Teenager.* New York: Bard, 1999.

Howe, Neil, and William Strauss. *Milllennials Rising: The Next Great Generation.* New York: Vintage, 2000.

Long, Jimmy. *Generating Hope: A Strategy for Reaching the Postmodern Generation.* Downer's Grove, IL: Intervarsity Press, 1997.

Lopiano-Misdom, Janine, and Joanne De Luca. *Street Trends: How Today's Alternative Youth Cultures Are Creating Tomorrow's Mainstream Markets.* New York: HarperBusiness, 1997.

Males, Mike A. *Framing Youth: Ten Myths about the Next Generation.* Monroe, ME: Common Courage Press, 1999.

Males, Mike A. *The Scapegoat Generation: America's War on Adolescents.* Monroe, ME: Common Courage Press, 1996.

Mitchell, Michele. *A New Kind of Party Animal: How the Young Are Tearing Up the American Political Landscape.* New York: Simon & Schuster, 1998.

Moses, Elissa. *The $100 Billion Allowance: How to Get Your Share of the Global Teen Market.* New York: John Wiley & Sons, 2000.

Olson, Lynn. *The School-to-Work Revolution: How Employers and Educators Are Joining Forces to Pre-pare Tomorrow's Skilled Workforce.* Reading, MA: Perseus Publishing, 1999.

Rainer, Thom S. *The Bridger Generation: America's Second Largest Generation, What They Believe, How to Reach Them.* Nashville, TN: Broadman & Holman Publishers, 1997.

Skelton, Tracey, and Gill Valentine. *Cool Places: Geographies of Youth Cultures.* London: Routledge, 1998.

Stevenson, David, and Barbara L. Schneider. *The Ambitious Generation: America's Teenagers, Motivated but Directionless.* New Haven, CT: Yale University Press, 2000.

Tapscott, Don. *Growing Up Digital: The Rise of the Net Generation.* New York: McGraw-Hill, 1999.

Tulgan, Bruce. *Managing Generation X.* New York: W.W. Norton, 2000. (First published Santa Monica, CA: Merritt, 1995).

Tulgan, Bruce. *The Manager's Pocket Guide to Generation X.* Amherst, MA: HRD Press, 1998.

Zemke, Ron, and Bob Filipczak. *Generations at Work: Managing the Clash of Veterans, Boomers, Xers, and Nexters in Your Workplace.* New York: AMACOM, 1999.